Guided Meditation for The Law of Attraction

Powerful Affirmations, Guided Meditation, and Hypnosis for Love, Money, Weight Loss, Relationships, and Happiness!

Olivia Clifford

© **Copyright 2021 - All rights reserved.**

The content contained within this book may not be reproduced, duplicated or transmitted without direct written permission from the author or the publisher.

Under no circumstances will any blame or legal responsibility be held against the publisher, or author, for any damages, reparation, or monetary loss due to the information contained within this book, either directly or indirectly.

Legal Notice:

This book is copyright protected. It is only for personal use. You cannot amend, distribute, sell, use, quote or paraphrase any part, or the content within this book, without the consent of the author or publisher.

Disclaimer Notice:

Please note the information contained within this document is for educational and entertainment purposes only. All effort has been executed to present accurate, up to date, reliable, complete information. No warranties of any kind are declared or implied. Readers acknowledge that the author is not engaged in the rendering of legal, financial, medical or professional advice. The content within this book has been derived from various sources. Please consult a licensed professional before attempting any techniques outlined in this book.

Table of Contents

Introduction

Chapter One: The Law Of Attraction

What Exactly is the Law of Attraction?

How Does the Law of Attraction Work?

7 Steps for Deliberate Attraction

Chapter Two: Guided Meditation

Benefits of Guided Meditation

Tips for Successful Guided Meditation

Guided Meditation Exercises

Guided Meditation Exercise to attract Good

Guided Meditation Exercise for Happiness

Guided Meditation Exercise for Money

Guided Meditation Exercise for Love & Relationships

Guided Meditation Exercise for Weight Loss

Key Takeaways

Chapter Three: Hypnosis

Hypnosis: A Recognized Form of Therapy

So, what is Hypnosis?

Tips for Using Hypnosis for Goal Achievement

Step by Step Guide for Self-hypnosis

Chapter Four: Self-Hypnosis Scripts

Suggestions for weight loss

Script to attract Money

Scripts for Happiness

Script to attract love and relationships

Script for Self-love and Confidence

Script for Success

Chapter Five: Powerful Affirmations For Self-Improvement

Affirmations for Happiness

Affirmations for Manifesting Money

Affirmations for Love

Positive Affirmations for Self-love

Powerful Affirmations for Relationships

Affirmations for Weight Loss

Positive Affirmations for Success

Conclusion

Key Takeaways

Introduction

Sometimes it can be so difficult to change your unwanted behaviors, attitudes, or situations. Have you ever wondered why? For instance, why can't addicted smokers just make one emphatic decision to stop smoking? Why can't you just decide once to stop anxiety and just relax more and enjoy life? Here is a quick revelation. Your mind has it all. One part of you agrees to change. And another part says "no way". It is like each of us has two minds which disagree on what should and shouldn't change.

Your mind is a very complex entity, and it is difficult to totally understand it. But, know that each of us has one mind with two different aspects — conscious and subconscious. Your conscious mind includes your current awareness. It is part of you that decides on what to do or where to go. Your subconscious is the part of your mind that works below the surface of your awareness. It has access to all your memories, holds your beliefs and values, and efficiently recalls all your frequently used behavior patterns. Your subconscious mind also runs the body functions like breathing, digestion, and many other tasks which you've never thought of.

Your subconscious and conscious mind work together. However, the subconscious mind is resistant to the sudden change that's why sometimes it appears to be working against the conscious mind. This is mainly because of "programming," especially when you attempt to change a longstanding habit, behavior, belief, or attitude.

Your mind is like a computer. Just like a computer has installed programs, so does your mind. Your behavioral sequence and thought patterns are examples of such 'programs'. You and others by other people (parents, teachers, peers, etc install some of these 'programs'.). We have a saying in computer programming—"Garbage in, garbage out." It simply means, if you input the wrong data in the computer, you will get the wrong output. Therefore, what you put in your mind is what you get or experience. If you feed your mind with negative thoughts and vibes, you get failure as an output.

Just like computer programs need to be activated with the right commands, so do your mind programs. Whenever a certain sequence of thoughts, words, or events occurs, your mind programs are ready and waiting in the subconscious mind to be activated. This usually works to your advantage, as it is the very essence of learning. However, sometimes you may realize that you input some garbage (negative thoughts and vibes) in your mind long ago and you no longer need them; you want to get rid of them. Perhaps you simply want to reprogram your mind by adding a new attitude, or behavior, that appeals to you.

Changing your subconscious mind's programs is not a simple thing. However, if you reprogram your subconscious mind, you can completely change your life. Your mind comes with a filter, a protector that acts as an inbuilt security system. This filter screens new thoughts, beliefs, and behaviors, ensuring that you want what you say you want. It is very slow for accepting sudden changes that are inconsistent with your old thoughts, behaviors, or beliefs.

Your subconscious mind is nondiscriminatory; this works to your benefit to keep your beliefs, behaviors, and personality consistent. Here, any idea or suggestion that is allowed past the mental filter is accepted as true. To avoid ending up in a state of confusion, the security system prevents you from changing your mind and accepting every suggestion that comes your way. However, this can be troublesome if you want to change something in your life for your good. The mind's security system can always reject ideas and even suggestions from your conscious thoughts. It can prevent you from reprogramming your mind with good ideas and positive vibes for change. It does this because it evaluates the new ideas, even good ones based on the previously accepted beliefs and interpretation of experience.

We have several ways to deal with the security system of your subconscious mind to enable change in your life. But, some ways are more expedient than others. Some people, for instance, repeat a new behavior until it becomes a habit. This method has its challenges but some iron-willed souls who persevere sometimes change themselves, because repeating an activity several times can override the subconscious mind's security system. Your inner mind eventually accepts the fresh ways of doing things and becomes a habit.

This book offers you powerful and preferable tools for change. It discusses the most expedient methods of reprogramming your mind. If you want to stay happy, lose weight, attract money, love and relationships, this book is for you. If you believe, it is going to help you rid yourself of all the negativity that has been holding you back. It starts by discussing the law of attraction, then it goes further and provides guided meditation exercises, affirmations, and self-hypnosis scripts for self-improvement. You only need to be committed to performing the exercises and you will never regret a single second spent on this book. Life is too short to spend it broken, miserable, and depressed. Here is the change you want and a solution to all your problems!

Chapter One: The Law of Attraction

Do you ever feel that sometimes things happen exactly how you want them to? The things that you need just fall into place or come to you from out-of-the-blues? Have you ever bumped into someone you were thinking about on the streets? Or a chance phone call from a lost friend just as you needed their help over something? Perhaps you've met your life partner or gotten your dream job just by fate or virtue of being at the right place at the right time. If you've ever experienced any of these, then you were experiencing the law of attraction. Some people find themselves in inappropriate relationships repeatedly. Perhaps your friend or relative has complained to you that they keep attracting the same kind (bad) of relationships. The law of attraction is at work for them as well. There is a fundamental force in the universe that guides people's lives and it is the underlying power behind all things—the law of attraction.

What Exactly is the Law of Attraction?

The law of attraction according to Napoleon Hill states that "we attract into our lives whatever we focus on". Put in simple terms, you get whatever you give your energy and attention to, be it positive or negative. The definition is simple but has a lot of meaning and truth in it. You are the one who creates your experiences, the surrounding people, the things that you receive, and your universe. You create them with the power of your thoughts.

This truth has spread to many people and has more recently been expressed in a popular quote:

Be careful with your thoughts, for they translate into words.

Be careful with your words, for they translate into actions.

Be careful of your actions, for they become habits.

Be careful of your habits, for they become character.

Be careful of your character, for it becomes your destiny.

The law of attraction tells us that whatever we give our attention to becomes what we magnetize into our lives.

How Does the Law of Attraction Work?

The basic premise of the law of attraction is "like attracts like". This means that two entities vibrating at the same frequencies pull towards each other. You can attract good things in your life when you have positive thoughts. The reverse is also true. Negative thoughts can bring you things that you don't want. You send out positive energy when you feel happy or loved. You send out negative energy when you feel bored, anxious, or stressed out.

Through the law of attraction, the universe responds enthusiastically to both vibrations. Based on the type of energy you create, it gives you more of it. It doesn't choose for you the best. Your energy vibrations attract the same frequencies back to you. Therefore, whatever you feel or think is your request to the universe for more of the same. Being aware of your energy, feelings, and thoughts are therefore very important. It helps you send out vibrations that resonate with what you want.

7 Steps for Deliberate Attraction

Know what you desire

Knowing exactly what you desire is key to attracting what you want. This gives the universe a simple time to act upon your desires. Most still don't know exactly what they truly want in life. The best way to desire something is to be specific.

You might say 'I would like more money, a good job, a good husband' however that's not enough. You must specify what you want.

'I would like a tall, handsome, stable, hardworking, loving, and respectful husband. I see myself walking with him along the beach and making love to each other'. Now, that is the proper way to know what you exactly want.

Be specific in your desires and visualize your emotions in your mind. The vibrations of your emotions are the ones that will make the law of attraction come alive.

Give your desire attention and ask the universe for it

The law of attraction gives you more of what you pay your attention to, put your energy and focus on. Meditate, and when you are calm, ask the universe for what you truly want. We are born in a universe where there are enough resources for everyone. The world "owes you a living". Your genuine desires are your "birth rights". But you have to know how to claim it.

Believe that they will come

The actual key to manifesting your desires is belief. It is very simple, it will not work for you if you don't believe it. You may say that I can't believe in something you cannot see. We have a solution for that: start small and remove any doubt. Act as if you already have it. Take moments out of your day-to-day life and re-experience what the sights and feelings are after you have been granted your desire. Just experience it as vividly as possible. The outcome will amaze you.

Use guided meditation to manifest your desires

Visualizing your desires in exact details can do wonders to your powers of manifestation. Your desires are brought to you a lot quicker if you visualize or use guided meditation to manifest them. Guided meditation is one of the best ways to infuse your mind. You take on a journey in your mind and help you to manifest the specific desire in your life. If you want something to happen in your life, think about it first. For instance, if you want an excellent partner, picture him/her in your mind, picture yourself enjoying life with the partner. You will see him/her and at long last, you have that life partner you wanted.

Inner dialogue

Be conscious of your inner dialogue and change the way you talk to yourself. Whatever you utter comes to pass. Your subconscious mind gets to work automatically and helps you make your desires real when you infuse your thoughts with what you desire in life. Using positive affirmations is one of the best ways to introduce new thoughts into your mind. If you practice positive thinking every day, your energy changes and attracts positive things in your life.

Allow it and Let go

Allowing is simply the absence of negative vibration, and any form of doubt is a negative vibration. You know you are allowing your desire when you hear yourself saying statements such as "Ah, what a relief!", "You know, maybe I can have this", or "Now this feels possible." Once you've set your desire in motion and allowed it, it is important to let go of your desire. Don't hold on to it too tight. Holding on to your desire too tight can kill it; it is like a butterfly. Hold on to it lightly and be free to enjoy life forever.

Thank the universe for granting your desire

Gratitude is very important in everything in life. Be grateful for everything you receive in life. Thank the universe for granting your desires. You infuse your thoughts and feelings with positive vibration energy when you practice gratitude in your daily life. This helps you to manifest more of your desires in life. The gratitude should come from your heart. Do it with passion, love, and positivity. Don't just do it in a rote fashion.

Now that you have learned about what the law of attraction is, how it works, and the steps involved in deliberate attraction, you now get more of what you want and less of what you don't want. This is not the end, we are going to learn more in the later chapters. The next chapter expounds more on guided meditation and provides you with exercises to help you attract money, love, relationships, happiness, and lose weight ASAP!

Chapter Two: Guided Meditation

Life treats us differently, but we all lead a hectic one. Nowadays, stress has become an inalienable part of our lives. Good enough, there are ways to control and prevent stress from getting to you. Meditation can help you with this. Meditation is the best way to order your life. Guided meditation is an effective paradigm that fits in with today's busy lifestyle. Using guided meditation techniques to reveal your life purpose is a deeply profound experience. It improves your creativity, health, wealth, and general quality of your life a thousand-fold.

Whether you have been practicing the law of attraction exercises for some time now or you are a novice, you probably know that meditation is an extremely powerful tool. You will hear people who have made it in life talk about the role of guided meditation. However, many manifestation books are shallow and skim over the details of this technique. They also cannot show you how to do it for specific goals.

In this chapter, we aim to tell you all you need to know. We will start by taking you through the benefits of guided meditation and the tips for successful manifestation meditation. Finally, we will show you how to perform specific guided meditation that attracts general good, love, money, relationships, happiness, and weight loss. If you are ready to attract all these, let's dive in!

Benefits of Guided Meditation

There are many benefits gained through meditation. Some of these benefits include stress relief, creativity stimulation, pain relief, sleep improvement, and positive influence on the state of mind. In this section, however, we are going to look at how meditation helps manifest and helps you to attract more positive vibes. Below are some ways you can use guided meditation for manifesting:

It helps you identify and overcome some of your manifestation blocks

For you to achieve your goals and be successful in life, know and overcome the blocks that are holding you back. Guided meditation is one of the most helpful tools in overcoming these manifestation blocks. Meditation helps you forget the outside world and completely switch off to listen to yourself.. You remove most of your abundance blocks. Guided meditations help you change your mindset and beliefs, thus steering your emotions and feelings in a more positive direction.

Guided meditation keeps you more aligned with the universe

Distraction and negative beliefs are the greatest enemies to a successful manifestation. Guided meditation helps you remove the distractions of the outside world and get into a flow state. Success in the law of attraction requires you to fully concentrate and focus on your goal. Guided meditations help you do just that.

Guided meditation trains your intuition and helps you take action

The law of attraction works only if you take action; it is not a magic formula. Through guided meditation, you can strengthen your intuition and attract creative ideas.

Guided meditation can help you become positive and attract more positive vibes

One rule of the law of attraction is "like attracts like". You need a positive attitude to manifest your dream life successfully. Try as much as possible to distance yourself from negative feelings and thoughts. Guided meditation can help you with that.

Guided meditation can help you visualize your dream life

One of the most powerful tools for the law of attraction is visualization; it helps you manifest faster and better. Sometimes you may struggle with visualizing your dreams and goals. In most cases, distractions will cause this. Guided meditation can be of great help here.

Tips for Successful Guided Meditation

Find a peaceful spot

Find a place that is comfortable and quiet; free from external distractions. While meditating, it is natural to find your mind wandering, especially for beginners. Noise and other forms of distraction can make it difficult for you to concentrate and center yourself. Your seating arrangement is also very important. Experiment with original positions to discover what relaxes you. Choose a seating position that calms you down and makes you comfortable.

Posture

Sitting cross-legged with your hands placed on your lap is the ideal posture for meditating. However, earlier, choose what is comfortable for you. Don't force yourself if it is not working for you. Choose a posture that you can manage in the beginning.

Focus

Narrow your focus by concentrating on your breathing. Breathing helps you calm down and prepare you for the actual meditation process. Master the technique of deep breathing and do it well. Notice how your chest rises and falls when breathing in and out, respectively. When distracted, don't judge yourself but gently return your attention to your breathing.

Visualize your desires

Picture what you want to attract using the full force of your imagination. Build this image using all senses. For example, if you're working to manifest money, how will it feel to hold in your arms? What will it smell like? What texture does the money have? Spend as much time building and inhabiting this image as you want.

Embrace your Gratitude

Picture the things that you already have and tune into a deep feeling of gratitude. This helps you attract more abundance into your life.

Finish with tranquility

Pay attention to your surroundings once you are ready to end the session. Notice the movements and the surrounding sounds. Sift your attention to your body to allow the integration to occur. Slowly open your eyes.

Guided Meditation Exercises

You now understand how guided meditation can be a shortcut to boosting your vibes and achieving your goals. You also know how to have a successful meditation session. Let's put it into practice.

Try as much as you can to set aside 15 minutes every day to perform these exercises.

Guided Meditation Exercise to attract Good

Find a comfortable and quiet place and sit comfortably. With your body relaxed and eyes closed, take a few slow, deep inhalations and exhalations.

Bring any recurring patterns to your awareness and take a few moments to observe the patterns and your reaction to them.

Start noticing the negative thoughts or beliefs that perpetuate the recurring patterns.

Next, ask your higher self to help you identify things that are contributing to your current situation.

Begin by bringing one major theme to your mind. Think of all the different moments in your life that this pattern has been present. Notice what happened to you during that time and where you were.

During that period, what was your mindset? What emotions and feelings did you experience?

How did you express yourself? What was your reaction to what was happening? Did something bring this pattern to an end?

What key takeaway do you have from this experience and your reactions to it? What lesson did you learn from the past that can help you activate the law of attraction to attract positive experiences in the future?

Now, let go of what is not helping you to clear out old wounds and beliefs from the past.

Imagine that you're bringing down healing from God, spirit, or the universe to heal you from inside and fill you with new positive energy.

Once you are filled with this healing energy, start visualizing the person, belief, or pattern that you want to dissolve. Imagine flowing this healing from your heart to your external being and ask it to be healed as well.

Say what is needed to say to bring this energy down. Ask your higher self to guide you and then imagine breaking the energetic cord that connects you to this situation and see it dissolved completely.

Now, manifest what you wanted to. Visualize it in the brightest, colorful, exciting, and joy-filled way. Act as if you already have it. Notice how happy you are and feel the positive emotions running through you. Be grateful for all the gifts this life has given upon you.

When you feel that what you're seeing is powerful and real, inhale deeply. As you breathe out, imagine energizing everything you have with this visual representation.

While still sitting, notice the internal shifts allowing the integration to occur. Slowly open your eyes when you are ready.

Guided Meditation Exercise for Happiness

Sit or lie down comfortably in a quiet place. Take a deep breath in and close your eyes as you exhale.

Take a moment and recall the intention for today's practice: to welcome happiness as your birthright.

Notice any negative thoughts and limiting beliefs that act against your happiness and release them to free yourself.

Take a moment and recall your heartfelt desire—happiness

Ask your higher self to guide you. Now manifest happiness. Visualize it in a joy-filled way.

Notice how happy you are, take in any important sounds, feel the positive vibrations running through you, and steep yourself in gratitude for the gift given to you.

Imagine yourself going about your day, welcoming in joy throughout.

When you feel this image is powerful and real, open and close your eyes several times whilst welcoming in joy.

Sit for a few more moments to notice the internal shifts allowing the integration to occur. Welcome yourself back to your open eyes and alert state of waking consciousness.

Guided Meditation Exercise for Money

Sit comfortably, close your eyes and take a deep breath in and out.

Open your heart and let go of any negative thoughts, beliefs, or anxiety.

Imagine yourself holding huge bundles of money.

Visualize yourself feeling the texture of the notes in your hands, rub them between your fingers, and imagine smelling them.

Imagine yourself matching your bank with your ATM card to withdraw a tremendous amount of money.

Picture yourself withdrawing the money. Imagine you've spent some of the money and are still comfortably well off. Give thanks and open your eyes slowly.

Guided Meditation Exercise for Love & Relationships

Sit or lie down comfortably in a quiet place. Take a deep breath in and close your eyes as you exhale.

Take a moment and recall the intention for today's practice: to find love as your birthright.

Notice any negative thoughts, limiting beliefs, or experiences that prevent you from falling in love. Release them to free yourself.

Take a moment and recall your heartfelt desire—to find the love of your life

Ask your higher self to guide you. Now manifest about them. Imagine how it would be to share your life with them.

Allow that feeling of calmness and completeness to fill you up.

Reflect on what it is to have everything that you need. Notice how happy you are, feel the positive energy running through you, and steep yourself in gratitude.

Imagine the light-emitting magnetic pull attracting others towards you.

When you feel this image is powerful and real. Take a deep breath in and out.

Sit for a few more moments to notice the internal shifts allowing the integration to occur. Welcome yourself back to your open eyes and alert state of waking consciousness.

Guided Meditation Exercise for Weight Loss

Sit or lie down comfortably in a quiet place. Take a deep breath in and close your eyes as you exhale.

Take a moment and recall the intention for today's practice: to become fat-free and fit.

Notice any negative thoughts or limiting beliefs that prevent you from losing weight. Release them to free yourself.

Take a moment and recall your heartfelt desire—to lose weight

Ask your higher self to guide you. Now it is about losing weight. Visualize yourself as beautiful and thinner.

Notice how fit, happy, and confident you are. Feel the positive energy running through you and steep yourself in gratitude.

Imagine yourself strutting around with confidence in those skinny dresses and trousers.

When you feel this image is powerful and real, take a deep breath in and out.

Sit for a few more moments to notice the internal shifts allowing the integration to occur. Welcome yourself back to your open eyes and alert state of waking consciousness.

Key Takeaways

- Early mornings are the best time for meditation
- Choose a peaceful place that is free from noise and distractions
- Your posture is crucial for a successful meditation session
- Focus is equally important. Count while breathing in and out if you find it difficult to focus on your breathing.
- Don't blame yourself or get upset when your mind drifts when meditating
- Always visualize your desires as you meditate
- Always embrace gratitude
- Ensure that you are filled with enthusiasm before starting your meditation journey

Chapter Three: Hypnosis

You must have heard of the term hypnosis. And, if you are like many other people, you must have heard of its effectiveness in helping people achieve their goals. You might even have thought of how you can use hypnosis to change your life. Maybe you would like to be hypnotized to improve your physical body to get lean and trim, find love and better relationships, get more money or stop smoking once and for all. Or, maybe you are stressed in your life and want to be hypnotized to release the tension and feel more relaxed. Who doesn't want to be happy? Who doesn't need love, good health, and wealth? Perhaps you've wondered if hypnosis could help with this. Yes, it can!

Hypnosis: A Recognized Form of Therapy

Hypnosis has been around since time immemorial. This phenomenon has been used as therapy. It was not until the 19th century that a man named Dr. James Braid coined it. Since then, the field of clinical hypnotherapy has been developing. The American Medical Association for inclusion in medical schools even approved hypnosis instruction in the late 1950s. Clinicians have then considered hypnosis a serious topic in the healing arts. Hypnosis is a safe and efficient tool for growth and self-improvement. It does not mean hypnosis for specific people, nearly everyone can be hypnotized. It is easy to learn and use. It doesn't require any fancy equipment to apply it. Once you understand the basic tenets and techniques, self-hypnosis can easily be applied; it is self-therapy that is free of cost. And unlike drug therapies, self-hypnosis does not have negative side effects. It is safe and friendly.

So, what is Hypnosis?

If you ask ten hypnotherapists for the definition of hypnosis, you will get over ten different answers. There is no consensus about the definition of hypnosis. Most of the definitions provided describe how hypnosis is induced rather than what it is. For the sake of instruction, here is a short but broad definition: Hypnosis is a state of narrowed focus in which suggestibility is greatly heightened.

While in this state, positive ideas, values, and images may be impressed upon your subconscious mind to elicit beneficial changes.

Tips for Using Hypnosis for Goal Achievement

1. **Visualize.** Program your subconscious mind with your desired outcome. During self-hypnosis, visually imagine that you have already accomplished your goal and reached your aim. See it as real and experience all the wonderful feelings associated with the attainment of that goal.

2. **Persistence**. Program your subconscious mind to change your inner character traits and have the traits of the people who never give up. Be persistent regardless of your current situation.

3. **Think Positive.** Program your subconscious mind to think positively and expect positive results. Your inner mind tends to replay the memories and throw them into consciousness as doubts and fears. You can eliminate this during self-hypnosis.

4. **Program out the Problem**. When trying to pursue worthwhile goals, inevitably, some problems will arise. You can solve these problems fairly rapidly through self-hypnosis. Just see yourself successfully traversing the obstacle while in a trance.

5. **Pre-pave your path.** Imagine yourself being in the right place at the right time, meeting the right people. Use the power of hypnosis to

program your mind like this. Your subconscious mind will pick up on non-verbal clues, process the millions of bits of information you receive every second, and guide you to the right course of action.

6. **Develop faith.** Convince your subconscious mind that your goal is already a reality. "Fake it till you make it". Use self-hypnosis to fool your subconscious mind into believing the "real" world is exactly like the world you have been visualizing.

Step by Step Guide for Self-hypnosis

1. **Make yourself comfortable:** Find a quiet and comfortable place to sit or lie. Have an open posture that is easy to maintain for at least 20 minutes. Take a few slow, deep breaths, allow your eyes to close naturally, and let your mind relax.

2. **Release any tension**: Release any physical tension throughout your body. Imagine each muscle is completely relaxing right from your toes, up to your legs, and on your back. Your shoulders and upper back hold a lot of tension, so spend extra time on them. Visualize your body gradually filling up with a calm, glowing light.

3. **Connect with your subconscious**: To successfully connect with your subconscious mind, roll your eyes back in your head gently and visualize yourself at the top of a staircase. You can imagine anything that can represent your consciousness. It doesn't have to be a staircase. Move your focus from your conscious mind at the top of the staircase to your subconscious at the bottom.

4. **Descend down the stairs slowly, taking one stair at a time**: With each stair take a slow, deep breath and let yourself feel even more relaxed than you did on the previous step, drifting deeper and deeper into your relaxing trance state. Start counting from 10 with each step going down until you get to 1 at the bottom of the staircase.

5. **Place your suggestions into your subconscious:** Once you reach the bottom of the staircase, start implanting hypnotic suggestions that resonate with your desired goal into your subconscious. You can gently repeat one or more of the following phrases in your mind:

    - "I am calm and relaxed"
    - "I do not fear anything"
    - "I am strong and confident"
    - "I now stop this bad habit"
    - "I am in control of my destiny"
    - "I deserve love"
    - "I can have everything I want"
    - "I deserve to have happiness in all areas of my life"
    - "I am healthy and energetic"
    - "I lose body fat safely and easily"
    - "I can remember my dreams"
    - "I feel safe becoming leaner"
    - "I am a lucid dreamer"
    - "I have a powerful drive and motivation to increase my monetary income"
    - Just remember to make every phrase positive and in the present tense.

6. **Wake Up Gently:** Repeat your chosen phrases as many times as you want. Enjoy the feeling of deep relaxation. Prepare to wake up from your trance state when you're ready. Tell yourself that you are going to count up to 10 as you climb up the stairs and with each step, you will slowly return to full awareness. Now start counting from 1 as you climb back up the steps in your mind. When you reach 10, take a deep breath and then open your eyes. Sit for a moment, then stand up slowly.

Chapter Four: Self-hypnosis Scripts

Before you recite any of these scripts, do the following to induct self-hypnosis environment:

- Find a quiet and comfortable place to sit or lie in an open posture that is easy to maintain for at least 20 minutes. Take a few slow, deep breaths, allow your eyes to close naturally, and let your mind relax.
- Tell yourself that you intend to make this a deep relaxation session.
- Take three deep breaths. Hold your breath for a couple of seconds after breathing in deeply before breathing out
- As you breathe in, imagine that you are taking in all the positive energy that the universe offers as calm, glowing light - feel this light filling up your body and helping you to relax.
- As you breathe out, imagine that the light is moving out of your body into the universe, taking with it all your stress, tension, worries, irritation, and anxieties.
- Starting from your toes, relax your body to your head. Tell that part of your body to relax. Don't force yourself to relax, just allow it to happen all by itself.
- It is now time to deepen your relaxation. Roll your eyes back in your head gently and visualize yourself at the top of a staircase.
- Descent down the stairs slowly, taking one stair at a time. With each stair take a slow, deep breath and let yourself feel even more relaxed than you did on the previous step, drifting deeper and deeper into your relaxing trance state. Start counting from 10 with each step going down until you get to 1 at the bottom of the staircase.
- Once you reach the bottom of the staircase, start implanting the hypnotic suggestions that best suit your desired goal.

Suggestions for weight loss

"I am worthy of having a healthy body and am worthy of being happy with how I look. I lose body fat safely and easily. I program my body and mind to change my body composition now so that I reduce my weight and become leaner each day. My body muscles increase now each day so that I can appear lean and attractive. I am becoming leaner now, my energy is increasing and I feel stronger and more important. I am comfortable and I will now move faster. As my body becomes leaner, I will become healthier. I will feel more confident as I am leaner. I deserve to feel and look good.

"I am a happy, confident person who is happy with my body. I see myself fitting into my smaller size clothes better. My body shape is more pleasing now. My self-esteem is high now. I see myself being active in everything that I do. The fat is still melting off me and I feel lighter.

"I imagine looking at my leaner image in a mirror. My body looks great. I imagine wearing new clothes that I just bought to fit my new body shape. I look good at them. I am so delighted by my body shape. My waist is smaller. I admit I look sexier with my current body composition. All the curves on my body are just in the right place. I look so good. I feel good seeing how lean and beautiful I look. It makes me feel free.

"I feel so in love with myself. I have peace of mind. I don't need food to feel comfortable. I no longer need to isolate myself from other people. I feel protected and secure by myself, and this feeling makes me eat the right foods in the right proportions.

"I will use food to nourish and fuel my body not to reward or entertain myself. Food is like fuel for my body. I will no longer use it to compensate for anything. I will fuel my body with the right food. So I stop myself from eating junk foods that could slow down my body. I will consume nutritious foods.

"Day by day I am losing weight and becoming beautiful and leaner. I feel safe and comfortable with my new appearance. I feel healthy. I feel a sense of freedom as I become healthier and leaner."

(The wake-up)

"I am going to count from 1 to 10. When I reach the number 10, I will be fully awake and alert. I begin. One...awakening from hypnosis. Two...becoming more awake. Three...becoming more conscious. Four...noticing my surroundings. Five...feeling satisfied. Six...feeling safe and comfortable. Seven...feeling more awake and full of health. Eight...looking forward to positive results from this hypnosis session. Nine...feeling wonderful and refreshed. TEN...TEN...TEN...now wide awake and fully alert." (Take a deep breath and then open your eyes. Sit for a moment then stand up slowly)

Script to attract Money

"I have the power and motivation to attract more money. " I now release any limiting beliefs about my ability to make money. I now choose to believe in myself to make more money. I will use this money in a good way. I can have more money and be more generous. I can afford to have the life I want when I have more money.

"I deserve to have anything that I can imagine. I live in a universe that is full of abundance. I allow myself to be a partaker of this abundance. I notice the abundance of wealth and money that is all around me, and I allow myself to flow with that abundance. I accept more money with joy and thanksgiving.

"I am now open to making more money. I see myself holding an immense sum of money. I imagine matching to the ATM to withdraw a vast amount of money. I see myself purchasing a luxurious house and car. I am wise in my decision to make and spend money. I draw the opportunities I need to attract and make more money.

"I can get what I want...yes, I can get what I want. I am smart enough to get anything I want in life. I now foster the thoughts, beliefs, and attitudes necessary to get more money. I now allow creativity and aggressiveness to guide me in generating more money."

(The wake-up)

"I am going to count from 1 to 10. When I reach the number 10, I will be fully awake and alert. I begin. One...starting to awaken from hypnosis. Two...becoming more awake. Three...starting to become more conscious. Four...becoming aware of my surroundings. Five...feeling satisfied. Six...feeling safe and comfortable. Seven...feeling more awake and full of health. Eight...looking forward to positive results from this hypnosis session. Nine...feeling wonderful and refreshed. TEN...TEN...TEN...now wide awake and fully alert." (Take a deep breath and then open your eyes. Sit for a moment then stand up slowly)

Scripts for Happiness

"I deserve to have happiness in all areas of my life. I now feel happy and content. Each day, I am becoming happier and more content. Other people's mistakes are not mine. I choose to be healthy and happy. Life is wonderful in every shape and form. I am now becoming a cheerful person with positive attitudes towards life.

"I will strive to partake of all the goods that come with the world. Every single day, I notice more and more of the good things in my life. The things that make me smile; the things that make me feel good on the inside; things that make me feel proud of myself. And as I notice more of these good things in my life every day, I become happier. As I become happier, it becomes easier for me to see more good things and become happier.

"My spirit is pure and with great joy; it continues to provide me with ultimate happiness. I acknowledge my superpowers and use them to facilitate more happiness. My life is made of joy. I am pure happiness personified."

(The wake-up)

"I am going to count from 1 to 10. When I reach the number 10, I will be fully awake and alert. I begin. One...starting to awaken from hypnosis. Two...becoming more awake. Three...starting to become more conscious. Four...becoming aware of my surroundings. Five...feeling satisfied. Six...feeling safe and comfortable. Seven...feeling more awake and full of health. Eight...looking forward to positive results from this hypnosis session. Nine...feeling wonderful and refreshed. TEN...TEN...TEN...now wide awake and fully alert." (Take a deep breath and then open your eyes. Sit for a moment then stand up slowly)

Script to attract love and relationships

"I deserve love, companionship, compassion, and empathy. The universe loves me and I can find love from the people in it. I can attract ideal people in my love. I release any limiting beliefs and past experiences that prevent me from getting into relationships. I decide now to let go of my feelings of irritation about love and relationships. I am no longer a prisoner of my past.

"I approach relationships with confidence and courage; not seeking what I can get from them, but what I can give to them. There is too much love in my relationship and this brings great joy in my life. I am happy to be in this relationship. I am loved by everyone around me and I continue to love them back in equal measure. I keep nurturing good relationships with the surrounding people. I keep working hard for my relationship. It can work.

"I am in love. I easily attract the right people into my life. I attract positive-minded people and repel those with negative minds. I love the people I attract. I walk a path of light and love. I want to be happy in my relationships. I acknowledge and love the people around me as they love me too."

(The wake-up)

"I am going to count from 1 to 10. When I reach the number 10, I will be fully awake and alert. I begin. One…starting to awaken from hypnosis. Two…becoming more awake. Three…starting to become more conscious. Four…becoming aware of my surroundings. Five…feeling satisfied. Six…feeling safe and comfortable. Seven…feeling more awake and full of health. Eight…looking forward to positive results from this hypnosis session. Nine…feeling absolutely wonderful and refreshed. TEN…TEN…TEN…now wide awake and fully alert." (Take a deep breath and then open your eyes. Sit for a moment then stand up slowly)

Script for Self-love and Confidence

"I love myself. I am so special and there is nobody else like me. I have self-worth and inner beauty. I like who I am and the person I am becoming. My life is so amazing. I love everything about myself. Every day, I grow and become a better version of myself. I praise myself and others naturally and effortlessly.

"I don't need to change anything about myself in order to be accepted and loved. I have a strong belief in myself. People look up to me in everything; they like my character and admire me. I am so grateful for my unique talents, achievements, and health.

"Every day, I am more and more aware of my innate beauty, creativity, and abundance. I am empowered to get the things that I seek. I can assert myself and stand up for myself and others as well. I naturally feel good about myself. Each day, I tap into my greatest potential. Love flows from within me. I love myself for what I am and all that I have accomplished. I believe in myself, my dreams, and my abilities. I am so grateful for everything I have achieved and for what I am yet to do."

(The wake-up)

"I am going to count from 1 to 10. When I reach the number 10, I will be fully awake and alert. I begin. One...starting to awaken from hypnosis. Two...becoming more awake. Three...starting to become more conscious. Four...becoming aware of my surroundings. Five...feeling satisfied. Six...feeling safe and comfortable. Seven...feeling more awake and full of health. Eight...looking forward to positive results from this hypnosis session. Nine...feeling absolutely wonderful and refreshed. TEN...TEN...TEN...now wide awake and fully alert." (Take a deep breath and then open your eyes. Sit for a moment then stand up slowly)

Script for Success

"I want to succeed with all my goals. Success is my portion. I have the determination of a bull and I am wise like an angel. I can succeed in whatever I put my mind to. Nothing can stop me from succeeding, no matter what comes my way. I am motivated to succeed. I know that success is achievable, and I am designed for it. I take action to open doors in my life.

"I know what I want in life, and I will go for it; I dare to put my mind and body to work for it. I now call upon allied forces to aid me in my quest. The universe is already on my side. I have support from all sides: above and below, left and right, in front and behind me.

"I remain silent about my goals. I will only share with those ready to assist me in achieving them directly. I know what I want, I don't need everyone's suggestions and comments. I believe I can have and achieve what I want. I remain silent about my goals until I achieve them.

"Nothing happens unless I make it happen. I will go towards success as it comes towards me. I take my next step towards achieving my ultimate goal. I see myself taking the next step."

(The wake-up)

"I am going to count from 1 to 10. When I reach the number 10, I will be fully awake and alert. I begin. One...starting to awaken from hypnosis. Two...becoming more awake. Three...starting to become more conscious. Four...becoming aware of my surroundings. Five...feeling satisfied. Six...feeling safe and comfortable. Seven...feeling more awake and full of health. Eight...looking forward to positive results from this hypnosis session. Nine...feeling absolutely wonderful and refreshed. TEN...TEN...TEN...now wide awake and fully alert." (Take a deep breath and then open your eyes. Sit for a moment then stand up slowly)

Chapter Five: Powerful Affirmations for Self-Improvement

Repeat the following affirmations three times every day for twenty-one days and see the change that comes your way.

Affirmations for Happiness

I deserve to be happy, and therefore I choose happiness

Today, I create peace, harmony, and joy in my heart

All my previous negative thoughts and self-images have disappeared

Other people's mistakes are not mine

I deserve to have happiness in all areas of my life

I am happy and calm right at this moment

I choose to be happy, feel happy, and have happy thoughts

I give up all negative thoughts and feelings about me

I have everything that I need to be happy about right now

From now henceforth, happiness is my constant state of mind

I am proud of what I have become

I choose to surround myself with happy people

I welcome all the good things the universe offers me

I am so grateful to the universe for all the blessings and good things in my life

From now on, everything is well, and my dreams are coming true every day

Living fully and freely is my birthright

Happiness is a choice, so I choose it

Being happy is becoming my habit day by day

Every time I breathe, I inhale the energy of happiness

My spirit is of great joy, and it continues to provide me with ultimate happiness.

Affirmations for Manifesting Money

Money is a tool that can fully change my life for better

I am worthy of financial security and all that this brings to me

I am magnetizing money and wealth to me in all forms and from all possible sources

Money flows to me effortlessly in various ways

Money is flowing into my life in large quantities from multiple sources NOW

I graciously accept the money that is flowing to me NOW

I expect more money to flow into my life in unexpected ways NOW

I am open and ready to receive more money from all sources NOW

I welcome large sums of money into my life regularly

The negative emotions about money do not serve my financial goals

I set my financial goals because I know I can achieve them

I am on the path to a wealthy life, poverty is not my portion

I have all it takes to be a financially successful person

I do not have any financial worries

Money is flowing to me like a river

I see my bank account figures increasing every single day

Every day I wake up, I get richer and richer

I am thankful for all the money that is present in my life now

Affirmations for Love

I am worthy of love and respect

I trust the universe, and I allow it to help me find genuine love

I give love and it is returned to me multiplied many times

My heart is always open to love

Everywhere I go, I naturally find love

I am surrounded by love; it is all around me

My thoughts are always loving, and my heart is full of love

Today I bless my being with infinite love

Every day my love grows stronger

My belief in love opens my heart to receiving it

All the love I need is within me

Today I choose to be loved and happy

I attract love easily and effortlessly

I deserve to be loved, and I allow myself to be loved

I am a magnet to love,

The more love I give, the more love I receive

Everything I do is in the vibration of love

I give unconditional love to everyone

My heart is filled with love

I deserve love, and I get it in abundance

As I share love with others, the universe gives back love to me

Today I free myself from fear of love, and I open my heart to welcome love

Positive Affirmations for Self-love

I love myself unconditionally

I choose myself today and forever

I respect and love myself for who I am

I embrace self-love as it flows through me

I deserve love; I know that self-love allows others to love me.

I am so proud of myself and my personal journey

I am beautiful in and out

I will stop apologizing for being myself

I am successful and I appreciate what I have in life right now

I am grateful for all my achievements and the gifts in my life

I am stronger because of my struggles

I have an open and loving heart

I am superior to negative thoughts and low actions

Many people look up to me and recognize my worth; I am admired.

I am enthusiastic, energetic and strong

I have the power to create the change I want in my life

I have a beautiful and healthy body, a brilliant mind, and tranquil soul

I have endless and unique talents that I begin to utilize from today

I have all the qualities needed in order to be extremely successful

I completely accept what I cannot change

I am so creative, talented, and original

Powerful Affirmations for Relationships

I attract lasting and happy relationships into my life

I naturally attract perfect relationships into my life

I only attract healthy relationships

My relationships are created in infinite love

I am now ready to accept a happy and lasting relationship

I appreciate every person I meet as worthy as my lover

I am attracting the right person for me

I deserve to be happy in my relationship

I trust the universe that it knows what kind of relationship I need in my life

I am in a wonderful relationship with people who treat me right

I deserve good people around me

All my connections are my significant and they fill me up

I practice and show kindness to everyone around me

My relationships are always fulfilling

I am grateful for the people I have in my life right now

I choose to surround myself only with people who are positive and who lift my energy

I am worth of the real relationship filled with love and respect

I deserve mind-blowing passion in my relationships

I am worth of a healthy, loving relationship

I am grateful for all the love and wonderful relationships in my life

Affirmations for Weight Loss

I deserve to be in perfect body shape

I deserve to have a slim, healthy and attractive body

I am clear about my fitness goals

I choose to embrace thoughts of confidence in my ability to for positive changes in my life

My body has an ideal weight and I have the perfect body shape

I am happy with every part I do in my significant efforts to lose weight

I am committed to my weight loss goal by changing my diet and eating habits from unhealthy to healthy.

I eat the right food for my body and I enjoy healthy food

It is exciting to discover my unique food for weight loss

My metabolism is running optimally, helping me achieve the body weight I desire

Every day I am getting slimmer, leaner and healthier

I exercise every day to enjoy a strong, toned body. I love the feeling exercise gives me

I am getting fitter, tonner and stronger everyday through exercise

I choose to exercise more and more

I am patient with creating my desired body shape and size

I look forward to achieving my ideal weight

I now clearly see myself at my ideal weight and body shape

Positive Affirmations for Success

I deserve to be successful

I am a strong person who attracts success

I am a magnet for success

I succeed in everything that I put my mind on

I have a healthy body, a brilliant mind and a tranquil soul

Everything that is happening in my life now is happening for my ultimate good

My potential to succeed is infinite

I am surrounded by supportive people who believe in me and want me to be successful

I have a limitless ability to conquer all the challenges I encounter

I have the potential to achieve great things in my life

I let go of all old, negative thoughts and beliefs that have stood in the way of my success

I choose to have positive thoughts and create wonderful and successful life that I want

The universe is full of abundance, I am prepared to receive success in abundance

I am passionate about constantly being better and more successful

I continue to climb higher for there is no limit to what I can achieve

Whatever I want comes to me when I go after it

I am so happy because all of my dreams are coming true

Great things are coming my way

I am successful in all areas of my life

Affirmations work when you continually remind your mind what you want to achieve. We live hectic lives that we even forget what we want in life and when opportunities present themselves, we often miss them because we are too busy to notice. To ensure that your affirmations work:

- State your affirmations in the positive
- Have faith. Convince your mind that you have it already
- Repeat your affirmations daily for at least 21 days or until you achieve your desired goal. People believe that it takes 21 days to develop a habit.
- Say your affirmations one at a time with enthusiasm.

Conclusion

The law of attraction through guided meditation, hypnosis and use of affirmations trains you to release the power that is within you. This technique is as old as humankind, yet a few have availed themselves of its benefits. This book teaches you how to use the law of attraction intelligently so that you, too, can realize your full potential in life and achieve your desired goals.

Self-hypnosis, guided meditation, and the use of positive affirmations can contribute positively to every phase of your life—physically, mentally, and spiritually. Do not make the mistake of our ancestors by underestimating the power of utilizing the law of attraction in these forms.

Using hypnosis and guided meditation to enhance life can be wonderful. Just from a suggestion, the mind can mold and create mental interpretations of sensations in ways that they had not been felt before. You can taste colors, feel textures, feel sounds, smell, and enhance the strength of a sensation far greater than you have before. The time has come for the law of attraction to come out of the closet. In your quest for self-improvement, you must try something different.

Key Takeaways

- Set a regular time every day to play or recite the scripts
- A quiet and peaceful place that is free from noise and distractions is these exercises
- Ensure that you are comfortable. Take a posture that makes you more comfortable.
- Release all the tension from your muscles before you start.
- Make well use of hypnosis induction scripts
- To maximize the effect, always repeat the suggestions frequently
- Have strong faith. Convince your subconscious mind that your goal is already a reality.
- Always use visualizations by mental movies to establish goals and empower yourself
- Ensure that you are filled with enthusiasm before starting any of these sessions
- Sometimes, it is natural for your conscious mind to wander during hypnosis or meditation sessions. Don't be concerned that you are wasting time and start blaming yourself, instead, keep focusing.
- Hypnosis, meditation, or rather the law of attraction, can be induced by anyone. It is not meant for specific persons.
- Never force yourself to enter a meditation or hypnosis session. Allow the willingness to come naturally. Vigorous efforts to enter these sessions prevent a successful response as much as strong resistance.
- Words have power, be careful of every word that comes from your mouth.
- Work on one goal or issue at a time.
- The more determined you are to attain a goal, the greater your chances of success
- To be the best subject to these techniques, you have to be more strong-willed, intelligent, and imaginative.

Most successful, powerful, wealthy, and famous people you hear of have used the law of attraction to be where they are. Motivation, discipline, persistence, and psychic empowerment are the most valuable qualities you can possess. Once this is established, solving problems is easy. Using guided meditation, self-hypnosis, and positive affirmations is the quickest and easiest road to your personal and professional growth. They are proven and natural methods for resolving problems quickly and easily.

You can achieve all your goals, change your life, and custom design your destiny using the simple exercises presented throughout this book. You don't need to rely on drugs and health professionals to treat your issues. Try these simple time-tested techniques to solve your problems.

If you enjoyed this book in anyway, an honest review is always appreciated!

www.ingramcontent.com/pod-product-compliance
Lightning Source LLC
Chambersburg PA
CBHW030046100526
44590CB00011B/344